PILOTS

CAREERS

William Russell

The Rourke Press, Inc.
Vero Beach, Florida 32964

Edited by Sandra A. Robinson

PHOTO CREDITS
© Lynn M. Stone: cover, title page, pages 10, 13, 21; courtesy of
United Airlines: pages 4, 7, 12, 15; courtesy of U.S. Air Force
Academy: page 8; courtesy of U.S. Navy Flight Demonstration
Squadron: pages 17, 18

Library of Congress Cataloging-in-Publication Data

Russell, William, 1942-
    Pilots / by William Russell.
    p. cm. — (Careers)
    Includes index.
    ISBN 1-57103-059-X
    1. Air pilots—Juvenile literature. [1. Air pilots. 2. Occupations.]
I. Title. II. Series: Russell, William, 1942-   Careers.
TL561.R85 1994
629.13'023—dc20   93-45009
                                                           CIP
Printed in the USA   AC

TABLE OF CONTENTS

PILOTS

Pilots are the men and women who fly aircraft — airplanes and helicopters. For **professional,** or paid, pilots, flying is their job.

Professional pilots may be hired to fly helicopters, small airplanes or big jets. A few professional pilots work as **flight instructors.** Flight instructors teach other people how to fly aircraft.

Military pilots are professional, too. They fly aircraft for the Army, Navy, Marines, Air Force and Coast Guard.

Professional pilots are well-trained men and women who are hired to fly aircraft

WHAT PILOTS DO

Most pilots fly for an airline. Airlines are companies that own and manage airplanes.

The pilot's job is to fly passengers from one place to another, and to get there on time. The airplane is used to carry people, goods known as air **cargo,** or both.

Pilots are trained so they can do their job in bad weather, poor light — or even darkness. Well-trained pilots can fly by using just their flight instruments to guide them!

An airline jet pilot checks a plane's tires during a pre-flight check called a "walkaround"

WHO CAN BE A PILOT?

Piloting aircraft is a demanding job. It requires many skills, steady nerves and good eyesight.

Pilots need to know how to fly an aircraft safely. They also must have knowledge of weather, **radar,** compasses, air communications and the aircraft's many systems.

Education is important for pilots. Some of the large airlines hire only college graduates.

A cadet studies flight at the United States Air Force Academy

WHERE PILOTS WORK

Pilots love to travel. A pilot's job may take him or her thousands of miles from home.

A professional jet pilot, for example, might begin the week in Chicago. On Tuesday he or she might fly 800 miles to New York. On Thursday, the pilot may fly 3,700 miles to Anchorage, Alaska.

Sooner or later, a pilot's flights take him or her back to the "home" airport.

Pilots enjoy a bird's-eye view of the land below them

Commercial jet pilots train on "simulators,"
which have control panels like those in real aircraft

Bush pilots haul passengers and cargo into remote places

COMMERCIAL PILOTS

Pilots who work for airlines that transport large numbers of people are **commercial** pilots. A commercial pilot spends most of a workday in the plane's **cockpit.** The cockpit is the pilot's control area in the front of the plane.

Commercial airplanes usually fly six or seven miles above the ground. The pilot has a great view on clear days.

A commercial pilot in the cockpit of a jet

MILITARY PILOTS

Pilots of military aircraft are part of the armed forces that keep the United States powerful. Many military aircraft are equipped with guns, bombs or rockets.

Military pilots fly for the U.S. government. They may fly in the United States or be sent to American air bases in other countries.

Military pilots fly sleek fighter planes, helicopters, heavy bombers and many other types of aircraft.

American military pilots fly some of the world's fastest, most modern jets

SOME SPECIAL PILOTS

Some pilots have especially exciting jobs. The U.S. Navy's Blue Angels fly in close, high-speed formations — patterns — at air shows. The Blue Angel pilots fly their F/A-18 Hornet fighters with breathtaking skill.

Other groups of Navy jet pilots take off from and land on the decks of huge, flat-topped ships called aircraft carriers.

The bush pilots of Alaska and Canada fly their little planes into rugged, **remote** places without runways.

Navy pilots of the Blue Angels demonstrate their skill in powerful, sleek F/A-18 Hornet fighter aircraft

THE PILOT'S HELPERS

Pilots depend on many people to help them fly safely. Air traffic controllers, for example, are pilots' radio contacts with airports on the ground.

Air traffic controllers follow the paths of airplanes on a radar screen. The controllers direct pilots to runways and air routes that are safe.

Mechanics keep airplanes healthy. They inspect and repair aircraft engines and bodies.

Air traffic controllers shuffle aircraft safely in and out of airports

LEARNING TO BE A PILOT

Pilot training begins with at least 20 hours of in-flight work. People who wish to be professional pilots continue training at flight schools and certain colleges.

The military services train pilots at several bases. Two of the best-known are the Pensacola Naval Air Station in Florida and the U.S. Air Force Academy in Colorado.

Glossary

cargo (KAR go) — the goods being transported; freight

cockpit (KAHK pit) — the area in an aircraft for the pilot and pilot controls

commercial (kuh MUR shul) — referring to actions or work that is done to earn money

flight instructor (FLITE in STRUK ter) — a person who teaches flying

professional (pro FESH un ul) — a person who is trained and paid for doing a job

radar (RAY dar) — an electronic system used to locate objects moving in the air

remote (re MOTE) — somewhere far away or out-of-the-way

INDEX